The Science of Getting Rich

by
Wallace D. Wattles

Updated for Today's World

by
Jeffrey L. King

CSJ King Publishing
Oregon, Wisconsin
Copyright © 2017 CSJ King Publishing
All rights reserved.

ISBN: 0-9856220-5-9
ISBN-13: 978-0-9856220-5-3

CONTENTS

PREFACE

This book is pragmatical, not philosophical; a practical manual, not a treatise upon theories. It is intended for the men and women whose most pressing need is for money; who wish to get rich first, and philosophize afterward. It is for those who have, so far, found neither the time, the means, nor the opportunity to go deeply into the study of metaphysics, but who want results and who are willing to take the conclusions of science as a basis for action, without going into all the processes by which those conclusions were reached.

It is expected that the reader will take the fundamental statements upon faith, just as he would take statements concerning a law of electrical action if they were promulgated by a Marconi or an Edison; and, taking the statements upon faith, that he will prove their truth by acting upon them without fear or hesitation. Every man or woman who does this will certainly get rich; for the science herein applied is an exact science, and failure is impossible. For the benefit, however, of those who wish to investigate philosophical theories and so secure a logical basis for faith, I will here cite certain authorities.

The monistic theory of the universe, the theory that One is All, and that All is One; That one Substance manifests itself as the seeming many elements of the material world, is of Hindu origin, and has been gradually winning its way into the thought of the western world for two hundred years. It is the foundation of all the Oriental philosophies, and of those of Descartes, Spinoza, Leibnitz, Schopenhauer, Hegel, and Emerson.

The reader who would dig to the philosophical foundations of this is advised to read Hegel and Emerson for himself.

In writing this book I have sacrificed all other considerations to plainness and simplicity of style, so that all might understand. The plan of action laid down herein was deduced from the conclusions of philosophy; it has been thoroughly tested, and bears the supreme test of practical experiment; it works. If you wish to know how the conclusions were arrived at, read the writings of the authors mentioned above; and if you wish to reap the fruits of their philosophies in actual practice, read this book and do exactly as it tells you to do.

Wallace D. Wattles
1910

Preface

My wife introduced me to Wallace Wattles' book "The Science of Getting Rich" as part of a personal and professional development course she teaches. As I started to read it, I realized there was a multitude of profound and useful ideas within these pages. After struggling through terminology and obscure references used in a literary work more than a hundred years old, I tried to share it with my young-adult daughter. She had difficulty relating to the message because of the archaic writing style. From that frustration grew the idea to do a "re-write" of the material for the 21st century, so that the life-changing ideas expressed could be better understood by a wider and more-modern audience.

In updating the terminology and examples used in this book, I strove to leave as much of Wattles' writing alone as I could. Indeed, there are many sentences and even entire paragraphs which I have left untouched. I have changed words or phrases here or there to make the concepts clearer and the examples more relative to today's audience. Wattles brings up industrial tycoons and monopolies, mistreatment of the working class, and other contemporary societal and economic issues. We live in a different age, with different issues facing us, and with a different perspective on the world and on life.

I've attempted to broaden the audience to make the language more inclusive than that used a hundred years ago, and to break from Wattle's singularly Christian perspective. Indeed, the messages contained within are important for every person on earth regardless of gender, race, religion, or economic status. All should read this book, hear its messages, and live its lessons.

Jeffrey L. King
2017

CHAPTER 1
THE RIGHT TO BE RICH

WHATEVER may be said in praise of poverty, the fact remains that it is not possible to live a really complete or successful life unless one has plenty of wealth. No one can rise to the greatest possible height in talent or soul development unless he has plenty of money; for to unfold the soul and to develop talent one must have many things to use, and one cannot have these things without the money to buy them.

A human develops in mind, soul, and body by making use of things, and our society and economy are so organized that we must have money in order to possess things; therefore, the basis of all advancement for humankind must be the science of creating wealth and getting rich.

The object of all life is to develop the skills and talents one has been given; and everyone has an inalienable right to all the development they are capable of attaining.

One's right to life means her right to have the free and unrestricted use of all the things which may be necessary to her fullest mental, spiritual, and physical advancement; or, in other words, her right to create wealth.

In this book, I shall not speak of riches in a figurative way; to be really rich does not mean to be satisfied or contented with a little. No one should be satisfied with a little if he is capable of using and enjoying more. The purpose of nature is the advancement and unfoldment of life; and everyone should have access to all that can contribute to the power, elegance, beauty, and richness of life. To be content with less is sinful because then we are not maximizing the wonderful potential that the Creator has given us all.

The person who owns all he wants for the living of all the life he is capable of living is rich; and anyone who has plenty of money can have all he wants. Life has advanced so far, and become so complex, that even the most ordinary man or woman requires a great amount of wealth in order to live in a manner that even approaches completeness. Every person naturally wants to become all that they are capable of becoming. This desire to realize innate possibilities is inherent in human nature; we cannot help wanting to be all that we can be. Success in life is becoming what you want to be. You can become what you want to be only by making use of things, but you can have things only as you become rich enough to buy them. To understand the science of getting rich is therefore the most essential of all knowledge.

There is nothing wrong with wanting to get rich. The desire for riches is really the desire for a richer, fuller, and more abundant life, and that desire is praiseworthy. The person who does not desire to live more abundantly is abnormal, and so the person who does not desire to have money enough to buy all he wants is abnormal.

There are three motives for which we live: we live for the body, we live for the mind, and we live for the soul. No one of these is better or holier than the other; all are desirable, and no one of the three — body, mind, or soul — can live fully if either of the others is cut short of full life and expression. It is not right or noble to live only for the soul and deny mind or body; and it is wrong to live for the intellect and deny body or soul.

We are all acquainted with the loathsome consequences of living for the body and denying both mind and soul, and we see that real life means the complete expression of all that we can give forth through body, mind, and soul. Whatever we can say, no one can be really happy or satisfied unless the body is living fully in every way, and unless the same is true of the mind and the soul. Wherever there is unexpressed possibility, or function not performed, or potential not achieved, there is unsatisfied desire. Desire is possibility seeking expression, function seeking performance, potential seeking achievement.

One cannot live fully in body without good food, comfortable clothing, and warm shelter, and without freedom from hard and excessive labor. Rest and recreation are also necessary to this physical life.

One cannot live fully in mind without books and time to study them, without opportunity for travel and observation, or without intellectual companionship.

To live fully in mind one must have intellectual recreations, and must surround oneself with all the objects of art and beauty one is capable of using and appreciating.

To live fully in soul, one must have love, but love is denied expression by poverty.

A person's highest happiness is found in sharing the benefits that have been reaped on those he loves. Love finds its most natural and spontaneous expression in giving. The person who has nothing to give cannot fill their place as a husband or father, wife or mother, as a citizen, or as a human. It is in the use of material things that one finds full life for the body, develops the mind, and unfolds the soul. It is therefore of supreme importance to that person that they should be rich.

It is perfectly right that you should desire to be rich; if you are a normal man or woman you cannot help but do so. It is perfectly right that you should give your utmost attention to the Science of Getting Rich, for it is the noblest and most necessary of all studies. If you neglect this study, you are derelict in your duty to yourself, to God, and to humanity, for you can give back to the Creator and humanity no greater gift than to make the most of yourself.

CHAPTER 2
THERE IS A SCIENCE OF GETTING RICH

THERE is a Science of getting rich, and it is an exact science, like algebra or arithmetic. There are certain laws which govern the process of acquiring riches; once these laws are learned and obeyed by any person, they will get rich with mathematical certainty.

The ownership of money and property comes as a result of doing things in a Certain Way; those who do things in this Certain Way, whether on purpose or accidentally, get rich, while those who do not do things in this Certain Way, no matter how hard they work or how able they are, remain poor.

It is a natural law that like causes always produce like results; and, therefore, any man or woman who learns to do things in this Certain Way will invariably get rich.

That the above statement is true is demonstrated by the following facts:

Getting rich is not a matter of environment, for, if it were, all the people in certain neighborhoods would become wealthy. The people of one community would all be rich, while those in other places would all be poor. The inhabitants of one region would roll in wealth, while those of an adjoining region would suffer in poverty.

But everywhere we see rich and poor living side by side, in the same environment, and often engaged in the same vocations. When two people are in the same place, and engage in the same business, and one gets rich while the other remains poor, it shows that getting rich is not primarily a matter of environment. Some environments may be more favorable than others, but when two people in the same business are in the same place, and one gets rich while the other fails, it indicates that getting rich is the result of doing things in a Certain Way.

And furthermore, the ability to do things in this Certain Way is not due solely to the possession of talent, for many people who have great talent remain poor, while other who have very little talent get rich.

Studying the people who have gotten rich, we find that they are average people in all respects, having no greater talents and abilities than other people. It is evident that they do not get rich because they possess talents and abilities that others do not have, but instead because they happen to do things in a Certain Way.

Getting rich is not the result of saving, or being thrifty. Many very miserly people who hoard what they get are poor, while free spenders often get rich.

Nor is getting rich due to doing things which others fail to do, for two people in the same business often do almost exactly the same things; one gets rich while the other remains poor or even becomes bankrupt.

From all these things, we must come to the conclusion that getting rich is the result of doing things in a Certain Way.

If getting rich is the result of doing things in a Certain Way, and if like causes always produce like results, then any man or woman who can do things in that way can become rich, and the whole matter is brought within the domain of exact science.

The question arises whether this Certain Way may not be so difficult that only a few may follow it. This cannot be true, as we have seen so far as natural ability is concerned. Talented people get rich, and those with few talents or skills get rich; intellectually brilliant people get rich, and very stupid people get rich; physically strong people get rich, and weak and sickly people get rich.

Some degree of ability to think and understand is, of course, essential; but as far as natural ability is concerned, any man or woman who has sense enough to read and understand these words can certainly get rich.

Also, we have seen that it is not a matter of environment, although location does count for something; one would not set up shop in the Sahara Desert and expect to do successful business.

Getting rich involves the necessity of dealing with other people, and being where there are people to deal with. And if these people are inclined to deal in the way you want to deal, so much the better. But that is about as far as environment goes.

If anybody else in your community can get rich, so can you; and if anybody else in your state or country can get rich, so can you.

Again, it is not a matter of choosing some particular business or profession. People get rich in every business, and in every profession, while their next-door neighbors in the same vocation remain in poverty.

It is true that you will do best in a business which you like, and which suits your personality. And if you have certain talents which are well developed, you will do best in a business which calls for the exercise of those talents.

Also, you will do best in a business which is suited to your locality; an ice cream parlor would do better in a warm climate than in Greenland, and a high-end restaurant will do better where there are plenty of customers who can afford to eat there.

But, aside from these general limitations, getting rich is not dependent upon your engaging in some particular business, but upon your learning to do things in a Certain Way. If you are now in business, and anybody else in your community is getting rich in the same business, but you are not getting rich, it is because you are not doing things in the same way as the other person.

No one is prevented from getting rich because they don't already have plenty of money. True, as you accumulate money, the increase becomes easier and faster; but one who has plenty of money is already rich, and does not need to consider how to become so. No matter how poor you may be, if you begin to do things in the Certain Way you will begin to get rich. You may be the poorest man on the continent, and be deeply in debt; you may not have any friends, influence, or resources. But if you begin to do things in this way, you must infallibly begin to get rich, for like causes must produce like results. If you have no material things, you can get material things. If you are in the wrong business, you can get into the right business. If you are in the wrong location, you can go to the right location. And you can do so by beginning in your present business and in your present location to do things in the Certain Way which leads to success.

Chapter 3
Is Opportunity Monopolized?

NO man is kept poor because opportunity has been taken away from him, because other people have monopolized the wealth, or because you are kept away from it. You may be shut off from engaging in business in certain lines, but there are other channels open to you. Probably it would be hard for you to build another great oil company or transportation company or fast-food chain; those fields are pretty well filled with plenty of successful businesses. But the internet is still in its infancy and offers almost infinite opportunities for enterprise, and the use of technology is expanding faster than we can keep up with it, so the opportunities for quickly building and growing a business are nearly endless. Why not focus on the future and turn your attention to the development of a new and innovative way to use technology, instead of competing with Exxon or Walmart or McDonald's, businesses that successfully developed their customer following decades ago?

It is quite true that if you work in fast food you have very little chance of becoming the owner of the chain for which you work. But it is also true that if you start to act in a Certain Way, you can soon leave what you see as a dead-end job; you can buy a website and domain name, and engage in a new business. There is great opportunity at this time for people to build a business from practically nothing and quickly become successful using technology and the internet; such people will certainly get rich. You may say that it is impossible for you to do this, but I am going to prove to you that it is not impossible, and that you can certainly build a better future if you will begin to think and work in a Certain Way.

At different times, the ship of opportunity sets sail in different directions, according to the needs of the whole of humankind, and the particular stage of social evolution which has been reached. In the past, one could become wealthy by participating in the industrial economy. Now that the developed nations have moved past the industrial economy, new wealth is usually related to technology and the internet. Today, opportunity is waiting for those with ideas for developing technology and internet-based businesses. Why limit yourself to selling to those only in your community when you can have the whole world using your product?

There is abundance of opportunity for those who will go with the tide, instead of trying to swim against it.

So the minimum wage workers, either as individuals or as a class, are not deprived of opportunity. The workers are not being "kept down" by their masters; they do not have any opportunities kept from them by those who control the economy. As a class, they are where they are because they do not do things in a Certain Way. If the working class chose to do so, they could follow the example of those who have already become rich, and establish great internet businesses and technology companies. They could elect people of their own class to office, and pass laws favoring entrepreneurialism; and in short order they could control their own destinies by being self-employed.

The working class may become the master class whenever they will begin to do things in a Certain Way; the law of wealth is the same for them as it is for all others. This they must learn: they will remain where they are as long as they continue to do as they do. The individual worker, however, is not held down by the ignorance or the mental slothfulness of his class; he can follow the tide of opportunity to riches, and this book will tell him how.

No one is kept in poverty by a shortness in the supply of riches; there is more than enough for all. The visible supply of money is practically inexhaustible; the invisible supply really IS inexhaustible. Wealth doesn't come from your employer; it comes to you through those with whom you do business.

Everything you see on earth, and beyond, is made from one original presence, out of which all things proceed. I will often call that presence "The Universal Mind" or the "Creator." You may refer to it in any way that fits your belief system: God, Allah, The Source of All, All That Is, The Universe, The Greater Intelligence, The Non-Physical, or whatever you choose. They are all different perspectives on the same thing.

New things are constantly being created, and older things are disappearing; but all are creations of The Universal Mind.

There is no limit to The Universal Mind. The universe is indeed made of it, but it was not all used up in the creation of the universe. The spaces in, through, and between the physical universe are filled with The Universal Mind, the formless stuff of ideas, the raw material that comprises all things. Ten thousand times as much as has been created might still be created, and even then we should not have exhausted the supply of universal raw material.

No one, therefore, is poor because nature is poor, or because there is not enough to go around.

The Universe is an inexhaustible storehouse of riches; the supply will never run short. The Universal Mind is alive with creative energy, and is constantly producing more forms. When the supply of building material or energy is exhausted, more will be produced. The Universal Mind responds to the needs and wants of mankind; it will not let mankind be without any good thing.

This is true of mankind collectively. The race as a whole is always abundantly rich, and if individuals are poor, it is because they do not follow the Certain Way of doing things which makes the individual person rich.

The Universal Mind is intelligent; it thinks, and responds to our wants and needs. It is alive, and is always impelled toward more life.

It is the natural and inherent impulse of life to seek to live more. It is the nature of intelligence to enlarge itself, and of consciousness to seek to extend its boundaries and find fuller expression. The universe has been made by The Universal Mind, creating physical form in order to express itself more fully.

The universe is a great living presence, always moving inherently toward more life and fuller functioning.

Nature is formed for the advancement of life; its impelling motive is the increase of life. For this cause, everything which can possibly help us to fulfill our lives is bountifully provided; there can be no lack of anything unless the Creator is to contradict itself and nullify its own works.

You are not kept poor by lack in the supply of riches. It is a fact which I shall demonstrate a little farther on that even the resources of The Universal Mind are at the command of every man or woman who will act and think in a Certain Way.

Chapter 4
The First Principle in The Science of Getting Rich

THOUGHT is the only power which can produce tangible riches from the The Universal Mind. The stuff from which all things are made is an intelligent presence which thinks, and our thoughts of form produce the form.

The Universal Mind moves according to its thoughts. Every form and process you see in nature is the visible expression of a thought in The Universal Mind. As The Universal Mind thinks of a form, it takes that form; as it thinks of a motion, it makes that motion. That is the way all things were created, and are still created. We live in a thought world, which is part of a thought universe. The thought of a moving universe extended throughout The Universal Mind, and The Universal Mind moving according to that thought, took the form of planets and galaxies, and maintains that form. The Universal Mind takes the form of its thought, and moves according to the thought. Holding the idea of a circling system of suns and worlds, it takes the form of these bodies, and moves them as it thinks. Thinking the form of a slow-growing oak tree, it moves accordingly, and produces the tree, though centuries may be required to do the work. In creating, The Universal Mind seems to move according to the lines of motion it has established; the thought of an oak tree does not cause the instant formation of a full-grown tree, but it does start in motion the forces which will produce the tree, along established lines of growth.

Every thought of form, held in The Universal Mind, causes the creation of the form, but always, or at least generally, along lines of growth and action already established.

The thought of a house of a certain construction, if it were impressed upon The Universal Mind, might not cause the instant formation of the house; but it would cause the turning of creative energies already working in trade and commerce into such channels as would result in the speedy building of the house. And if there were no existing channels through which the creative energy could work, then the house would be formed directly from The Universal Mind, without waiting for the slow processes of the physical world.

No thought of form can be impressed upon The Universal Mind without causing the creation of the form.

Mankind is a thinking center, and can originate thought. All the forms that mankind fashions with its hands must first exist in its thought; one cannot shape a thing until one has thought that thing.

And so far mankind has primarily confined its efforts wholly to the work of its hands; people have applied manual labor to the world of forms, seeking to change or modify what already exists. Mankind has seldom thought of trying to cause the creation of new forms by impressing its thoughts upon The Universal Mind.

When a person has a thought, they take material from the forms of nature, and make an image of the form which is in the mind. Mankind has, so far, made little or no effort to co-operate with The Universal Mind. Mankind has not dreamed that it can do what it sees The Universal Mind doing. Mankind reshapes and modifies existing forms by manual labor; it has given scant attention to the question whether it may not produce things from The Universal Mind by communicating human thoughts to it. We propose to prove that he may do so; to prove that any man or woman may do so, and to show how. As our first step, we must lay down three fundamental propositions.

First, we assert that there is one original Universal Mind from which all things are made. All the seemingly many elements are but different presentations of one substance; all the many forms found in organic and inorganic nature are but different shapes, made from the same stuff. And this stuff is thinking stuff; a thought held in it produces the form of the thought. Non-physical thought produces the physical manifestation of that thought. Mankind is a thinking center, capable of original thought; if mankind can communicate our thoughts to The Universal Mind, it can cause the creation, or formation, of the thing that is thought about.

To summarize this:

There is a Universal Mind from which all things are made, and which, in its original state, permeates, penetrates, and fills the interspaces of the universe.

A thought produces the thing that is imaged by the thought.

Mankind can form things in its thought, and, by impressing its thought upon The Universal Mind, can cause the thing to be created.

It may be asked if I can prove these statements; and without going into details, I answer that I can do so, both with logic and experience.

Reasoning back from the phenomena of form and thought, I come to one original Universal Mind; and reasoning forward from this Universal Mind, I come to mankind's power to cause the formation of the thing that is thought about.

And by experiment, I find the reasoning true, and this is my strongest proof.

If one person who reads this book gets rich by doing what it tells her to do, that is evidence in support of my claim. But if every person who does what it tells him or her to do gets rich, that is positive proof until someone goes through the process and fails. The theory is true until the process fails; and this process will not fail, for every person who does exactly what this book tells him or her to do will most certainly get rich.

I have said that people get rich by doing things in a Certain Way; and in order to do so, people must become able to think in a Certain Way.

A person's way of doing things is the direct result of the way he thinks about things.

To do things in a way you want to do them, you will have to acquire the ability to think the way you want to think; this is the first step toward getting rich.

To think what you want to think is to think truth, regardless of appearances.

Every person has the natural and inherent power to think what he wants to think, but it requires far more effort to do so than it does to think the thoughts which are suggested by appearances. To think according to appearance is easy; to think truth regardless of appearances is more difficult, and requires the expenditure of more power than any other work man is called upon to perform.

There is no task from which most people shrink as they do from that of sustained and consecutive thought; it is the hardest work in the world. This is especially true when truth is contrary to appearances. Every appearance in the visible world tends to produce a corresponding form in the mind which observes it; and these paradigms can only be prevented by holding the thought of the truth.

To look upon the appearance of disease will produce the form of disease in your own mind, and ultimately in your body, unless you hold the thought of the truth, which is that there is no disease present. It is only an appearance, and the reality is health.

To look upon the appearances of poverty will produce corresponding forms in your own mind, unless you hold to the truth that there is no poverty; there is only abundance.

To think health when surrounded by the appearances of disease, or to think riches when in the midst of appearances of poverty, requires power. But the one who acquires this power becomes a master mind. That person can conquer fate, and can have whatever they want.

This power can only be acquired by getting hold of the basic fact which is behind all appearances: that there is one Universal Mind, from which and by which all things are made.

Then we must grasp the truth that every thought held in The Universal Mind becomes a form, and that mankind can so impress its thoughts upon it as to cause them to take form and become visible things.

When we realize this, we lose all doubt and fear, for we know that we can create what we want to create. We can get what we want to have, and can become what we want to be. As a first step toward getting rich, you must believe the three fundamental statements given previously in this chapter, and in order to emphasize them, I repeat them here:

There is a Universal Mind from which all things are made, and which, in its original state, permeates, penetrates, and fills the interspaces of the universe.

A thought produces the thing that is imaged by the thought.

Mankind can form things in its thought, and, by impressing its thought upon The Universal Mind, can cause the thing to be created.

You must lay aside all other concepts of the universe than this monistic one; and you must dwell upon this until it is fixed in your mind, and has become your habitual thought. Read these statements over and over again; write them down again and again. Fix every word upon your memory, and meditate upon them until you firmly believe what they say. If a doubt comes to you, cast it aside as a sin. Do not listen to arguments against this idea; do not go to churches or lectures where a contrary concept of things is taught or preached. Do not read magazines or books which teach a different idea; if you get mixed up in your faith, all your efforts will be in vain.

Do not ask why these things are true, or speculate as to how they can be true; simply take them on trust.

The science of getting rich begins with the absolute acceptance of this faith.

Chapter 5
Increasing Life

YOU must get rid of the last vestige of the old idea that there is a God whose will it is that you should be poor, or whose purposes may be served by keeping you in poverty.

The Universal Mind which is All, and in All, and which lives in All and lives in you, is a consciously living presence. Being a consciously living presence, it must have the nature and inherent desire of every living intelligence for increase of life. Every living thing must continually seek for the enlargement of its life, because life, in the mere act of living, must increase itself.

A seed, dropped into the ground, springs into activity, and in the act of living produces a hundred more seeds. Life, by living, multiplies itself. It is forever becoming more. It must do so, if it continues to be at all.

Intelligence likewise needs continuous increase. Every thought we think makes it necessary for us to think another thought; consciousness is continually expanding. Every fact we learn leads us to the learning of another fact; knowledge is continually increasing. Every talent we cultivate brings to the mind the desire to cultivate another talent. We are subject to the urge of life, seeking expression, which ever drives us on to know more, to do more, and to be more.

In order to know more, do more, and be more, we must have more; we must have things to use, for we learn, and do, and become, only by using things. We must get rich, so that we can live more.

The desire for riches is simply the capacity for larger life seeking fulfillment. Every desire is the effort of an unexpressed possibility to come into action. It is power seeking to manifest which causes desire. That which makes you want more money is the same as that which makes the plant grow; it is life, seeking fuller expression.

The one Universal Mind must be subject to this inherent law of all life. It is filled with the desire to live more; that is why it needs to create things.

The Universal Mind desires to live more in you; hence it wants you to have all the things you can use.

It is the desire of God that you should get rich. She wants you to get rich because she can express herself better through you if you have plenty of things to use in giving her expression. She can live more in you if you have unlimited command of the means of life.

The Universe desires you to have everything you want to have.

Nature is friendly to your plans.

Everything is naturally for you.

Make up your mind that this is true.

It is essential, however, that your purpose should harmonize with the purpose that is in All.

You must want real life, not mere pleasure of sensual gratification. Life is the performance of function; and the individual really lives only when he performs every function, physical, mental, and spiritual, of which he is capable, without excess in any.

You do not want to get rich in order to live swinishly, for the gratification of animal desires; that is not life. But the performance of every physical function is a part of life, and no one lives completely who denies the impulses of the body a normal and healthful expression.

You do not want to get rich solely to enjoy mental pleasures, to get knowledge, to gratify ambition, to outshine others, to be famous. All these are a legitimate part of life, but the person who lives for the pleasures of the intellect alone will only have a partial life, and will never be satisfied with his lot.

You do not want to get rich solely for the good of others, to lose yourself for the salvation of mankind, to experience the joys of philanthropy and sacrifice. The joys of the soul are only a part of life; and they are no better or nobler than any other part.

You want to get rich in order that you may eat, drink, and be merry when it is time to do these things; in order that you may surround yourself with beautiful things, see distant lands, feed your mind, and develop your intellect; in order that you may love others and do kind things, and be able to play a good part in helping the world to find truth. All of these should be your reasons to get rich.

But remember that extreme altruism is no better and no nobler than extreme selfishness; both are mistakes.

Get rid of the idea that God wants you to sacrifice yourself for others, and that you can secure his favor by doing so. God requires nothing of the kind.

What the Universe wants is that you should make the most of yourself, for yourself, and for others; and you can help others more by making the most of yourself than in any other way.

You can make the most of yourself only by getting rich; so it is right and praiseworthy that you should give your first and best thought to the work of acquiring wealth.

Remember, however, that the desire of The Universal Mind is for all, and its movements must be for more life to all. It cannot be made to work for less life to anyone, because it is equally in all, seeking riches and life.

The Universal Mind will make things for you, but it will not take things away from someone else and give them to you.

You must get rid of the thought of competition. You are to create, not to compete for what is already created.

You do not have to take anything away from anyone.

You do not have to drive sharp bargains.

You do not have to cheat, or to take advantage. You do not need to let anyone work for you for less payment than they earn.

You do not have to covet the property of others, or to look at it with wishful eyes. No others have anything of which you cannot also have, and that without taking what they have away from them.

You are to become a creator, not a competitor. You are going to get what you want, but in such a way that when you get it every other person will also have more than they have now.

I am aware that there are people who get a vast amount of money by doing just the opposite as the statements in the paragraph above, and I will add a word of explanation here. People who become very rich do so sometimes purely by their extraordinary ability to compete against others, and sometimes they unconsciously relate themselves to The Universal Mind in its great purposes and movements for the general advancement of mankind. The great industrialists, like Rockefeller, Carnegie, and Morgan, have been the unconscious agents of The Universal Mind in the necessary work of systematizing and organizing productive industry; and over time, their work has contributed immensely toward increased life for all. They have organized production for all of us, and over time were succeeded by those who organized distribution for the great mass of consumers.

Those multi-millionaires are like the dinosaurs; they played a necessary part in the evolutionary process of mankind, but the same power which produced them will dispose of them. And it is well to bear in mind that those who gained by competing with others for resources were never really rich; a record of the private lives of most of the wealthy industrialists show that they were really the most abject and wretched of the poor.

Riches secured on the competitive plane are never satisfactory and permanent; they are yours today, and another's tomorrow. Remember, if you are to become rich in a scientific and certain way, you must rise entirely out of the competitive thought. You must never think for a moment that the supply is limited. Just as soon as you begin to think that all the money is being cornered and controlled by banks or multinational conglomerates, and that you must exert yourself to get laws passed to stop this process, you drop into the competitive mind, and your power to create for yourself is gone for the time being. And worse yet, you will probably stop the creative processes you have already begun.

Know that there are countless millions of dollars' worth of gold in the mountains of the earth, not yet brought to light; and know that if there were not, more would be created from The Universal Mind to supply your needs.

Know that the money you need will come, even if it is necessary for a thousand men to be led to the discovery of new gold mines tomorrow.

Never look at the visible supply; look always at the limitless riches in The Universal Mind, and know that they are coming to you as fast as you can receive and use them. Nobody, by cornering the visible supply, can prevent you from getting what is yours.

So never allow yourself to think for an instant that all the best building spots will be taken before you get ready to build your house, unless you hurry. Never worry about the banks and conglomerates, and get anxious for fear they will soon come to own the whole earth. Never be afraid that you will lose what you want because some other person beats you to it. That cannot possibly happen; you are not seeking anything that is possessed by anybody else. You are causing what you want to be created from The Universal Mind, and the supply is without limits. Stick to the formulated statement:

There is a Universal Mind from which all things are made, and which, in its original state, permeates, penetrates, and fills the interspaces of the universe.

A thought produces the thing that is imaged by the thought.

Mankind can form things in its thought, and, by impressing its thought upon The Universal Mind, can cause the thing to be created.

Chapter 6
How Riches Come to You

WHEN I say that you do not have to drive sharp bargains, I do not mean that you do not have to drive any bargains at all, or that you are above the necessity for having any dealings with other people. I mean that you will not need to deal with them unfairly. You do not have to get something for nothing, but can give to everyone more than you take from them.

You cannot give everyone more in cash market value than you take from them, but you can give them more in use value than the cash value of the thing you take from them. The paper, ink, and other material in this book may not be worth the money you pay for it; but if the ideas suggested by it bring you thousands of dollars, you have not been wronged by those who sold it to you. They have given you a great use value for a small cash value.

Let us suppose that I own a painting by a great artist. I take it to a family living in poverty and convince them to give me $500 for it. I have really wronged that family, for they have no use for the painting. It has no use value to them; it will not add to their lives.

But suppose I charge them for seeds and access to a garden plot and teach them how to grow their own vegetable garden; then they have made a good bargain. They have use for a vegetable garden; they will be able to grow their own food, which will add to their lives in every way. It will help make them rich.

When you rise from the competitive to the creative plane, you can examine your business transactions very strictly, and if you are selling anyone anything which does not add more to their life than the thing they gave you in exchange, you can afford to stop it. You do not have to beat anybody in business. And if you are in a business which does beat people, get out of it at once.

Give every person more in use value than you take from them in cash value; then you are advancing the life of the world with every business transaction.

If you have people working for you, you must take from them more in cash value than you pay them in wages; but you can so organize your business that it will be filled with the principle of advancement, and so that each employee who wishes to do so may advance a little every day.

You can make your business do for your employees what this book is doing for you. You can so conduct your business that it will be a sort of ladder, by which every employee who will take the trouble may climb to riches himself, and given the opportunity, if he will not do so it is not your fault.

And finally, because you are to cause the creation of your riches from The Universal Mind which permeates all your environment, it does not follow that they are to take shape out of thin air and come into being before your eyes.

If you want a new computer, for instance, I do not mean to tell you that you are to impress the thought of a computer on The Universal Mind until the machine is formed without hands and appears magically in the room where you sit. But if you want a new computer, hold the mental image of it with the most positive certainty that it is being made and is on its way to you. After once forming the thought, have the most absolute and unquestioning faith that the computer is coming. Never think of it, or speak of it, in any other way than as being sure to arrive. Claim it as already yours.

It will be brought to you by the power of the Supreme Intelligence, acting upon the minds of other men and women. If you live in Canada, it may be that someone will be brought from Texas or Japan to engage in some transaction which will result in your getting what you want.

If so, the whole matter will be as much to that person's advantage as it is to yours.

Do not forget for a moment that The Universal Mind is through all, in all, communicating with all, and can influence all. The desire of The Universal Mind for fuller life and better living has caused the creation of all the computers already made. It can cause the creation of millions more, and will, whenever someone sets it in motion by desire and faith, and by acting in a Certain Way.

You can certainly have a new computer in your house; and it is just as certain that you can have any other things which you want, and which you will use for the advancement of your own life and the lives of others.

You need not hesitate about asking largely. The Universal Mind wants to live all that is possible in you, and wants you to have all that you can use for the living of the most abundant life.

If you fix upon your consciousness the fact that the desire you feel for the possession of riches is one with the desire of The Universal Mind for more complete expression, your faith becomes invincible.

Once I saw a little boy sitting at a piano, and vainly trying to bring harmony out of the keys; and I saw that he was frustrated and upset by his inability to play real music. I asked him the cause of his frustration, and he answered, "I can feel the music in me, but I can't make my hands go right." The music in him was the urge of The Universal Mind, containing all the possibilities of all life. All that there is of music was seeking expression through the child.

The Universal Mind is trying to live and do and enjoy things through humanity. It is saying, "I want hands to build wonderful structures, to play divine harmonies, to paint glorious pictures. I want feet to run my errands, eyes to see my beauties, tongues to tell mighty truths and to sing marvelous songs," and so on.

All that there is of possibility is seeking expression through mankind. The Universal Mind wants those who can play music to have pianos and every other instrument, and to have the means to cultivate their talents to the fullest extent. It wants those who can appreciate beauty to be able to surround themselves with beautiful things. It wants those who can discern truth to have every opportunity to travel and observe. It wants those who can appreciate fashion to be beautifully clothed, and those who can appreciate good food to be luxuriously fed.

The Universal Mind wants all these things because it is itself that enjoys and appreciates them. The Universal Mind wants to play, and sing, and enjoy beauty, and proclaim truth, and wear fine clothes, and eat good foods.

The desire you feel for riches is The Universal Mind seeking to express itself in you as it sought to find expression in the little boy at the piano.

So you need not hesitate to ask largely.

Your part is to focus on what you want and express that desire to The Universal Mind.

This is a difficult point with most people; they retain something of the old idea that poverty and self-sacrifice are pleasing to God. They look upon poverty as a part of the plan, a necessity of nature. They have the idea that God has finished His work, and made all that He can make, and that the majority of men must stay poor because there is not enough to go around. They hold on to so much of this erroneous thought that they feel ashamed to ask for wealth; they try not to want more than a very modest amount of anything, just enough to make them fairly comfortable.

I recall now the case of one student who was told that he must get in mind a clear picture of the things he desired, so that the creative thought of them might be impressed on The Universal Mind. He was a very poor man, living in a rented house, and having only what he earned from day to day, and he could not grasp the fact that all wealth was his. So, after thinking the matter over, he decided that he might reasonably ask for a new rug for the floor of his best room, and a coal-burning stove to heat the house during cold weather. Following the instructions given in this book, he obtained these things in a few months; and then it dawned upon him that he had not asked enough. He went through the house in which he lived, and planned all the improvements he would like to make in it. He mentally added a bay window here and a room there, until it was complete in his mind as his ideal home; and then he planned its furnishings.

Holding the whole picture in his mind, he began living in the Certain Way, and moving toward what he wanted; and he owns the house now, and is rebuilding it after the form of his mental image. And now, with still larger faith, he is going on to get greater things. It has been given to him according to his faith, and it is so with you and with all of us.

Chapter 7
Gratitude

THE illustrations given in the last chapter conveyed to the reader the fact that the first step toward getting rich is to convey the idea of your wants to The Universal Mind.

This is true, and you will see that in order to do so it becomes necessary to relate yourself to The Universal Mind in a harmonious way.

To secure this harmonious relationship is a matter of such primary and vital importance that I shall give some space to its discussion here, and give you instructions which, if you will follow them, will be certain to bring you into perfect unity of mind with God and the Universe.

The whole process of mental adjustment and atonement can be summed up in one word: gratitude.

First, you believe that there is one Supreme Intelligence, from which all things proceed. Second, you believe that this intelligence gives you everything you desire. And third, you relate yourself to it by a feeling of deep and profound gratitude.

Many people who order their lives rightly in all other ways are kept in poverty by their lack of gratitude. Having received one gift from God, they cut the wires which connect them by failing to acknowledge what they have been given.

It is easy to understand that the nearer we live to the source of wealth, the more wealth we shall receive; and it is easy also to understand that the soul that is always grateful lives in closer touch with God than the one which never looks to God in thankful acknowledgment.

The more gratefully we fix our minds on The Universal Mind when good things come to us, the more good things we will receive, and the more rapidly they will come. The reason simply is that the mental attitude of gratitude draws the mind into closer touch with the source from which the blessings come.

If it is a new thought to you that gratitude brings your whole mind into closer harmony with the creative energies of the universe, consider it well, and you will see that it is true. The good things you have already received came to you along the line of obedience to certain laws. Gratitude will lead your mind out along the ways by which things come; and it will keep you in close harmony with creative thought and prevent you from falling into competitive thought.

Gratitude alone can keep you looking toward the All, and prevent you from falling into the error of thinking of the supply as limited; and to do that would be fatal to your hopes.

There is a Law of Gratitude, and it is absolutely necessary that you should observe the law, if you are to get the results you seek.

The law of gratitude is the natural principle that action and reaction are always equal, and in opposite directions.

The grateful outreaching of your mind in thankful praise to the Supreme is a liberation or expenditure of force; it cannot fail to reach that to which it is addressed, and the reaction is an instantaneous movement towards you — a reaction from the Supreme back to you. This is a statement of psychological truth.

And if your gratitude is strong and constant, the reaction in The Universal Mind will be strong and continuous. The movement of the things you want will be always toward you. Notice the grateful attitude that Jesus took; how He always seems to be saying, "I thank Thee, Father, that Thou hearest me." You cannot exercise much power without gratitude; for it is gratitude that keeps you connected with power.

But the value of gratitude does not consist solely in getting you more blessings in the future. Without gratitude you cannot for very long keep from being dissatisfied with things as they are.

The moment you permit your mind to dwell with dissatisfaction upon things as they are, you begin to lose ground. You fix your attention upon the common, the ordinary, the poor, and the squalid and mean; and your mind takes the form of these things. Then you will transmit these forms or mental images to The Universal Mind, and the common, the poor, the squalid, and mean will come to you.

To permit your mind to dwell upon the inferior is to become inferior and to surround yourself with inferior things.

On the other hand, to fix your attention on the best is to surround yourself with the best, and to become the best.

The Creative Power within us makes us into the image of that to which we give our attention.

We are thinking beings, and thinking beings always take the form of that which they think about.

The grateful mind is constantly fixed upon the best; therefore it tends to become the best. It takes the form or character of the best, and will receive the best.

Also, faith is born of gratitude. The grateful mind continually expects good things, and expectation becomes faith. The reaction of gratitude upon one's own mind produces faith; and every outgoing wave of grateful thanksgiving increases faith. He who has no feeling of gratitude cannot long retain a living faith, and without a living faith you cannot get rich by the creative method, as we shall see in the following chapters.

It is necessary, then, to cultivate the habit of being grateful for every good thing that comes to you, and to give thanks continuously.

And because all things have contributed to your advancement, you should include all things in your gratitude.

Do not waste time thinking or talking about the shortcomings or wrong actions of rich people or those who appear to control the economy. Their organization of the world has created your opportunity; all you get really comes to you because of them.

Do not rage against corrupt politicians. If it were not for politicians we should fall into anarchy, and your opportunity would be greatly lessened.

The Universal Mind has worked a long time and very patiently to bring us up to where we are in business and government, and The Universal Mind's work continues to go on. There is not the least doubt that those in control of the economy, business leaders, and politicians will be done away with as soon as they can be spared. But in the meantime, see that they are all necessary. Remember that they are all helping to arrange the lines of transmission along which your riches will come to you, and be grateful to them all. This will bring you into harmonious relations with the good in everything, and the good in everything will move toward you.

Chapter 8
Thinking in the Certain Way

TURN back to Chapter 6 and read again the story of the man who formed a mental image of his house, and you will get a fair idea of the initial step toward getting rich. You must form a clear and definite mental picture of what you want; you cannot transmit an idea unless you have it yourself.

You must have it before you can give it; and many people fail to impress their thoughts upon The Universal Mind because they have themselves only a vague and misty concept of the things they want to do, to have, or to become.

It is not enough that you should have a general desire for wealth "to do good with"; everybody has that desire.

It is not enough that you should have a wish to travel, see things, live more, etc. Everybody has those desires also. If you were going to send a text message to a friend, you would not send the letters of the alphabet in their order, and let him construct the message for himself; nor would you take words at random from the dictionary. You would send a coherent sentence, one which meant something. When you try to impress your wants upon The Universal Mind, remember that it must be done by a coherent statement; you must know what you want, and define it well. You can never get rich, or start the creative power into action, by sending out unformed longings and vague desires.

Go over your desires just as the man I have described went over his house; see just what you want, and get a clear mental picture of it as you wish it to look when you get it. Visualize the end product as you want it to be.

That clear mental picture you must have continually in mind, as the sailor has in mind the port toward which he is sailing his ship; you must keep your face toward it at all times. You must no more lose sight of it than the navigator loses sight of the compass.

It is not necessary to conduct exercises in concentration, or to set apart special times for prayer and affirmation, or to silently meditate, or to practice occult stunts of any kind. Those things have their purposes, but all you need is to know what you want, and to want it badly enough so that it will stay in your thoughts.

Spend as much of your leisure time as you can in contemplating your image, but no one needs special training to concentrate his mind on a thing which he really wants. It is the things you do not really care about which require effort to fix your attention upon them.

And unless you really want to get rich, so much that the desire is strong enough to continuously hold your thoughts, it will hardly be worthwhile for you to try to carry out the instructions given in this book.

The methods herein set forth are for people whose desire for riches is strong enough to overcome mental laziness and the love of ease, and make them work.

The more clear and definite you make your image then, and the more you dwell upon it, bringing out all its delightful details, the stronger your desire will be; and the stronger your desire, the easier it will be to hold your mind fixed upon the image of what you really want.

Something more is necessary, however, than merely to see the image clearly. If that is all you do, you are only a dreamer, and will have little or no power to accomplish anything.

Behind your clear vision must be the determination to realize it, to make it happen.

And behind this determination must be an invincible and unwavering faith that the thing is already yours, that it is yours for the asking, and you have only to take possession of it.

Live in the new house, mentally, until it takes form around you physically. In your thoughts, enter at once into full enjoyment of the things you want.

See the things you want as if they were actually around you all the time; see yourself as owning and using them. Make use of them in imagination just as you will use them when they are your tangible possessions. Dwell upon your mental image until it is clear and distinct, and then take the mental attitude of ownership of everything in that image. Take possession of it, in mind, in the full faith that it is actually yours. Hold to this mental ownership; do not waiver for an instant in the faith that it is real.

And remember what was said in the preceding chapter about gratitude: be as thankful for it all the time as you expect to be when it has taken form. The man who can sincerely thank God for the things which as yet he owns only in imagination, has real faith. He will get rich; he will cause the creation of whatever he wants.

You do not need to pray repeatedly for things you want; it is not necessary to remind God about it every day.

Your job is to intelligently formulate your desire for the things which make for a larger life, and to get these desires arranged into a coherent whole, and then to impress this whole desire upon The Universal Mind, which has the power and the will to bring you what you want.

You do not make this impression by repeating strings of words; you make it by holding the vision with unshakable determination, and with steadfast faith that you will attain it.

The answer to prayer is not according to your faith while you are talking, but according to your faith while you are doing.

You cannot impress The Universal Mind by having a special Sabbath day set apart to tell Him what you want, and then forgetting Him during the rest of the week. You cannot impress The Universal Mind by having special hours to go into your closet and pray, if you then dismiss the matter from your mind until the hour of prayer comes again.

Verbal prayer is well enough, and has its effect, especially upon yourself, in clarifying your vision and strengthening your faith; but it is not your oral petitions which get you what you want. In order to get rich you do not need a "sweet hour of prayer"; you need to "pray without ceasing." And by prayer I mean holding steadily to your vision, with the purpose to cause its creation into solid form, and the faith that you are doing so.

When you have formed your image, it is well to verbally thank the Supreme in reverent prayer; and from that moment you must, in your mind, receive what you ask for. Live in the new house; wear the fine clothes; ride in the automobile; go on the journey, and confidently plan for greater journeys. Think and speak of all the things you have asked for in terms of actual present ownership. Imagine an environment and a financial condition exactly as you want them, and live all the time in that imaginary environment and financial condition. Mind, however, that you do not do this as a mere dreamer and castle builder; hold to the faith that the imaginary is being realized, and to the determination to realize it. Remember that it is faith and determination in the use of the imagination which make the difference between the doer and the dreamer. And having learned this fact, it is here that you must learn the proper use of the will.

Chapter 9
How to Use the Will

TO set about getting rich in a scientific way, you do not try to apply your willpower to anything outside of yourself.

Your have no right to do so, anyway.

It is wrong to apply your will to other men and women, in order to get them to do what you wish done.

It is as flagrantly wrong to coerce people by mental power as it is to coerce them by physical power. If compelling people by physical force to do things for you reduces them to slavery, compelling them by mental means accomplishes exactly the same thing; the only difference is in methods. If taking things from people by physical force is robbery, then taking things by mental force is robbery also; there is no difference in principle.

You have no right to use your willpower upon another person, even for his own good, for you do not know what is for his good. The science of getting rich does not require you to apply power or force to any other person, in any way whatsoever. There is not the slightest necessity for doing so; indeed, any attempt to use your will upon others will only defeat your purpose.

You do not need to apply your will to things, in order to compel them to come to you.

That would simply be trying to coerce God, and would be foolish and useless, as well as irreverent.

You do not have to compel God to give you good things, any more than you have to use your willpower to make the sun rise.

You do not have to use your willpower to conquer an unfriendly deity, or to make stubborn and rebellious forces do your bidding.

The Universal Mind is friendly to you, and is more anxious to give you what you want than you are to get it.

To get rich, you need only to use your willpower upon yourself.

When you know what to think and do, then you must use your will to compel yourself to think and do the right things. That is the legitimate use of the will in getting what you want — to use it in holding yourself to the right course. Use your will to keep yourself thinking and acting in the Certain Way.

Do not try to project your will, or your thoughts, or your mind out into space, to control things or people.

Keep your mind at home; it can accomplish more there than elsewhere.

Use your mind to form a mental image of what you want, and to hold that vision with faith and purpose; and use your will to keep your mind working in the Right Way.

The more steady and continuous your faith and purpose, the more rapidly you will get rich, because you will make only positive impressions upon The Universal Mind; and you will not neutralize or offset them by negative impressions.

The image of your desires, held with faith and purpose, is taken up by The Universal Mind, and permeates it to great distances throughout the universe.

As this impression spreads, all things are set moving toward its realization; every living thing, every inanimate thing, and the things yet uncreated, are stirred toward bringing into being that which you want. All force begins to be exerted in that direction; all things begin to move toward you. The minds of people, everywhere, are influenced toward doing the things necessary to the fulfilling of your desires, and they work for you, unconsciously.

But you can check all this by starting a negative impression in The Universal Mind. Doubt or unbelief is as certain to start a movement away from you as faith and purpose are to start one toward you. It is by not understanding this that most people who try to make use of thoughts in getting rich fail. Every moment you spend in giving heed to doubts and fears, every moment you spend in worry, every moment in which your soul is possessed by unbelief, sets a current away from you in the whole domain of The Universal Mind. All the promises will come to them who believe, and to them only.

Since belief is all-important, it behooves you to guard your thoughts, and as your beliefs will be shaped to a very great extent by the things you observe and think about, it is important that you should command your attention.

And here the will comes into use; for it is by your will that you determine what things your attention shall be fixed upon.

If you want to become rich, you must not make a study of poverty.

Things are not brought into being by thinking about their opposites. Health is never to be attained by studying disease and thinking about disease; righteousness is not to be promoted by studying sin and thinking about sin; and no one ever got rich by studying poverty and thinking about poverty.

Medicine as a science of disease has increased disease; religion as a science of sin has promoted sin, and economics as a study of poverty will fill the world with wretchedness and want.

Do not talk about poverty; do not investigate it, or concern yourself with it. Nevermind what its causes are; you have nothing to do with them.

What concerns you is the cure.

Do not spend your time in charitable work, or charity movements; all charity only tends to perpetuate the wretchedness it aims to eradicate.

I do not say that you should be hard hearted or unkind, and refuse to hear the cry of need; but you must not try to eradicate poverty in any of the conventional ways. Put poverty behind you, and put all that pertains to it behind you, and get rich; that is the best way you can help the poor.

And you cannot hold the mental image to make you rich if you fill your mind with pictures of poverty. Do not read books or papers which give circumstantial accounts of the wretchedness of the homeless, of the horrors of those living in slums, and so on. Do not read anything which fills your mind with gloomy images of want and suffering.

You cannot help the poor in the least by knowing about these things. The proof is here: the widespread knowledge of poverty has done nothing to rid the world of it.

What tends to do away with poverty is not the getting of pictures of poverty into your mind, but getting pictures of wealth into the minds of the poor.

You are not deserting the poor in their misery when you refuse to allow your mind to be filled with pictures of that misery.

Poverty can be done away with, not by increasing the number of well-to-do people who think about poverty, but by increasing the number of poor people who determine to get rich.

The poor do not need charity; they need inspiration. Charity only sends them a loaf of bread to keep them alive for a few more hours in their wretchedness, or distracts them from their poverty for an hour or two; but inspiration will cause them to rise out of their misery. If you want to help the poor, demonstrate to them that they can become rich. Prove it by getting rich yourself.

The only way in which poverty will ever be banished from this world is by getting a large and constantly increasing number of people to practice the teachings of this book.

People must be taught to become rich by creation, not by competition.

Every man who becomes rich by competition throws down behind him the ladder by which he rises, and keeps others down; but every man who gets rich by creation opens a way for thousands to follow him, and inspires them to do so.

You are not showing hardness of heart or an unfeeling disposition when you refuse to pity poverty, see poverty, read about poverty, or think or talk about it, or to listen to those who do talk about it. Use your willpower to keep your mind off the subject of poverty, and to keep it fixed with faith and purpose on the vision of what you really want.

Chapter 10
Further Use of the Will

YOU cannot retain a true and clear vision of wealth if you are constantly turning your attention to opposing pictures, whether they be external or imaginary.

Do not tell of your past troubles of a financial nature, if you have had them; do not think of them at all. Do not tell of the poverty of your parents, or the hardships of your early life; to do any of these things is to mentally class yourself with the poor for the time being, and it will certainly check the movement of things in your direction.

Put poverty and all things that pertain to poverty completely behind you.

You have accepted a certain theory of the Universe as being correct, and are resting all your hopes of happiness on its being correct; and what can you gain by giving heed to conflicting theories?

Do not read religious books which tell you that the world is soon coming to an end; and do not read the rantings of the media or those on the internet who tell you that the world is a hellish place.

The world is not going to the devil; it is going to God.

It is transforming into something new and wonderful.

True, there may be a good many things at present which are disagreeable; but what is the use of studying them when they are certainly passing away, and when the study of them only tends to check their passing and keep them with us? Why give time and attention to things which are being replaced through evolutionary growth, when you can hasten their removal only by promoting evolutionary growth as far as your part of it goes?

No matter how horrible the conditions in certain places may seem, you waste your time and destroy your own chances by considering them.

You should interest yourself in the world becoming rich.

Think of the riches the world is coming into, instead of the poverty it is growing out of, and bear in mind that the only way in which you can assist the world in growing rich is by growing rich yourself through the creative method — not the competitive one.

Give your attention wholly to riches; ignore poverty.

Whenever you think or speak of those who are poor, think and speak of them as those who are becoming rich; as those who are to be congratulated rather than pitied. Then they and others will catch the inspiration, and begin to search for the way out.

Because I say that you are to give your whole time and mind and thought to riches, it does not follow that you are to be sordid or mean.

To become really rich is the noblest aim you can have in life, for it includes everything else.

On the competitive plane, the struggle to get rich is a Godless scramble for power over others; but when we come into the creative mind, all this is changed.

All that is possible in the way of greatness and soul unfoldment, of service and lofty endeavor, comes by way of getting rich; all is made possible by the use of things.

If you lack for physical health, you will find that the attainment of it is conditional on your getting rich.

Only those who are emancipated from financial worry, and who have the means to live a care-free existence and follow hygienic practices, can have and retain health.

Moral and spiritual greatness is possible only to those who are above the competitive battle for existence; and only those who are becoming rich on the plane of creative thought are free from the degrading influences of competition. If your heart is set on domestic happiness, remember that love flourishes best where there is refinement, a high level of thought, and freedom from corrupting influences; and these are to be found only where riches are attained by the exercise of creative thought, without strife or rivalry.

You can aim at nothing so great or noble, I repeat, as to become rich; and you must fix your attention upon your mental vision of riches, to the exclusion of all that may tend to dim or obscure the vision.

You must learn to see the underlying truth in all things. You must look beneath all seemingly wrong conditions and see the Supreme One always moving forward, toward fuller expression and more complete happiness.

It is the truth that there is no such thing as poverty; there is only wealth.

Some people remain in poverty because they are ignorant of the fact that there is wealth for them; and these can best be taught by showing them the way to affluence by your example.

Others are poor because, while they feel that there is a way out, they are too intellectually lazy to put forth the mental effort necessary to find that journey and travel it; and for these the very best thing you can do is to arouse their desire by showing them the happiness that comes from being rightly rich.

Others still are poor because, while they have some notion of science, they have become so swamped and lost in the maze of metaphysical and occult theories that they do not know which road to take. They try a mixture of many systems and fail in all. For these, again, the very best thing to do is to show the right way by example; an ounce of doing things is worth a pound of theorizing.

The very best thing you can do for the whole world is to make the most of yourself.

You can serve God and man in no more effective way than by getting rich, but only if you get rich by the creative method and not by the competitive one.

Another thing. We assert that this book gives in detail the principles of the science of getting rich; and if that is true, you do not need to read any other book upon the subject. This may sound narrow and egotistical, but consider: there can be but one shortest distance between two points. There is only one way to think scientifically, and that is to think in the way that leads by the most direct and simple route to the goal. No man has yet formulated a briefer or less complex system than the one set forth herein; it has already been stripped of all non-essentials. Lay all other ideas aside; put them out of your mind altogether.

Read this book every day; keep it with you, commit it to memory, and do not think about other systems and theories. If you do, you will begin to have doubts and be uncertain and wavering in your thought; and then you will begin to fail.

After you have made good and become rich, you may study other systems as much as you please; but until you are quite sure that you have gained what you want, do not read anything on this subject but this book, unless it be the authors mentioned in the Preface.

And read only the most optimistic comments on the world's news, those in harmony with your image of how things will be.

Also, postpone your investigations into the occult. It is very likely that the dead still live, and are near; but if they are, let them alone and mind your own business.

Wherever the spirits of the dead may be, they have their own work to do, and their own problems to solve, and we have no right to interfere with them. We cannot help them, and it is very doubtful whether they can help us, or whether we have any right to trespass upon their time if they can. Let the dead and the hereafter alone, and solve your own problem: get rich. If you begin to get involved with the occult, you will start mental cross currents which will surely dash your hopes upon the rocks. Now, this and the preceding chapters have brought us to the following statement of basic facts:

There is a Universal Mind from which all things are made, and which, in its original state, permeates, penetrates, and fills the interspaces of the universe.

A thought produces the thing that is imaged by the thought.

Mankind can form things in its thought, and, by impressing its thought upon The Universal Mind, can cause the thing it thinks about to be created.

In order to do this, you must pass from the competitive to the creative mind; you must form a clear mental picture of the things you want, and hold this image in your thoughts with fixed determination to get what you want, and the unwavering faith that you do get what you want, closing your mind against all that may tend to shake your purpose, dim your vision, or quench your faith.

And in addition to all this, we shall now see that we must live and act in a Certain Way.

Chapter 11
Acting in the Certain Way

THOUGHT is the creative power, or the impelling force which causes the creative power to act. Thinking in a Certain Way will bring riches to you, but you must not rely upon thought alone, paying no attention to personal action. That is the rock upon which many otherwise scientific metaphysical thinkers become shipwrecked — the failure to connect thought with personal action.

We have not yet reached the stage of development, even supposing such a stage to be possible, in which man can create directly from The Universal Mind without nature's processes or the work of human hands. People must not only think, but their personal action must supplement their thought.

By thought you can cause the gold in the hearts of the mountains to be impelled toward you; but it will not mine itself, refine itself, or come rolling down the road in the form of coins seeking the way into your pocket.

Under the impelling power of The Universal Mind, mankind's affairs will be so ordered that someone will be led to mine the gold for you; other people's business transactions will be so directed that the gold will be brought toward you, and you must so arrange your own business affairs that you may be able to receive it when it comes to you. Your thought makes all things, animate and inanimate, work to bring you what you want; but your personal activity must be such that you can rightly receive what you want when it reaches you. You are not to take it as charity or steal it; you must give every man more in use value than he gives you in cash value.

The scientific use of thought consists of forming a clear and distinct mental image of what you want, of holding fast to the purpose to get what you want, and in realizing with grateful faith that you do get what you want.

Do not try to project your thought in any mysterious or occult way, with the idea of having it go out and do things for you; that is wasted effort, and will weaken your power to think productively.

The action of thought in getting rich is fully explained in the preceding chapters: your faith and purpose positively impress your vision upon The Universal Mind, which has the same desire for more life that you have. And this vision, received from you, sets all the creative forces at work in and through their regular channels of action, but directed toward you.

It is not your part to guide or supervise the creative process; all you have to do with that is to retain your vision, stick to your purpose, and maintain your faith and gratitude.

But you must act in a Certain Way, so that you can appropriate what is yours when it comes to you; so that you can meet the things you have in your image, and put them in their proper places as they arrive.

You can really see the truth of this. When things reach you, they will be in the hands of other people, who will ask for something in return.

And you can only get what is yours by giving the other person what is his.

Your pocketbook is not going to be transformed into an overflowing treasure chest, which shall be always full of money without effort on your part.

This is the crucial point in the science of getting rich: right here, where thought and personal action must work together. There are very many people who, consciously or unconsciously, set the creative forces in action by the strength and persistence of their desires, but who remain poor because they do not provide for the reception of the thing they want when it comes.

By thought, the thing you want is brought to you; by action you receive it.

Whatever your action is to be, it is evident that you must act NOW. You cannot act in the past, and it is essential to the clearness of your mental vision that you dismiss the past from your mind. You cannot act in the future, for the future is not here yet. And you cannot tell how you will want to act in any future contingency until that contingency has arrived.

Because you are not in the right business or the right environment now, do not think that you must postpone action until you get into the right business or environment. And do not spend time in the present thinking about the best course in possible future emergencies; have faith in your ability to meet any emergency when it arrives.

If you act in the present with your mind on the future, your present action will be with a divided mind, and will not be effective.

Put your whole mind into acting in the present.

Do not give your creative impulse to The Universal Mind, and then sit down and wait for results; if you do, you will never get them. Act now. There is never any time but now, and there never will be any time but now. If you are ever to begin to prepare yourself for the reception of what you want, you must begin now.

And your action, whatever it is, must most likely be in your present business or employment, and must be upon the persons and things in your present environment.

You cannot act where you are not, you cannot act where you have been, and you cannot act where you are going to be; you can act only where you are.

Do not bother as to whether yesterday's work was well done or ill done; do today's work well.

Do not try to do tomorrow's work now; there will be plenty of time to do that when you get to it.

Do not try, by occult or mystical means, to act on people or things that are out of your reach.

Do not wait for a change of environment before you act; get a change of environment by action.

You can so act upon the environment in which you are now, as to cause yourself to be transferred to a better environment.

Hold with faith and purpose the vision of yourself in the better environment, but act upon your present environment with all your heart, and with all your strength, and with all your mind.

Do not spend any time in daydreaming; hold to the one vision of what you want, and act NOW.

Do not cast about seeking some new thing to do, or some strange, unusual, or remarkable action to perform as a first step toward getting rich. It is probable that your actions, at least for some time to come, will be those you have been performing for some time past; but you are to begin now to perform these actions in the Certain Way, which will surely make you rich.

If you are engaged in some business, and feel that it is not the right one for you, do not wait until you get into the right business before you begin to act.

Do not feel discouraged, or sit down and lament because you are in the wrong place. No one was ever so misplaced that they could not find the right place, and no one ever became so involved in the wrong business that they could not get into the right business.

Hold the vision of yourself in the right business, with the intent to get into it, and the faith that you will get into it, and are getting into it; but ACT in your present business. Use your present business as the means of getting a better one, and use your present environment as the means of getting into a better one. Your vision of the right business, if held with faith and purpose, will cause the Supreme to move the right business toward you. And your action, if performed in the Certain Way, will cause you to move toward that business.

If you are an employee, or wage earner, and feel that you must change places in order to get what you want, do not project your thought into space and rely upon it to get you another job. It will probably fail to do so.

Hold the vision of yourself in the job you want, while you act with faith and purpose in the job you have, and you will certainly get the job you want.

Your vision and faith will set the creative force in motion to bring it toward you, and your action will cause the forces in your own environment to move you toward the place you want. In closing this chapter, we will add another statement to our main points:

There is a Universal Mind from which all things are made, and which, in its original state, permeates, penetrates, and fills the interspaces of the universe.

A thought produces the thing that is imaged by the thought.

Mankind can form things in its thought, and, by impressing its thought upon The Universal Mind, can cause the thing it thinks about to be created.

In order to do this, you must pass from the competitive to the creative mind; you must form a clear mental picture of the things you want, and hold this image in your thoughts with fixed determination to get what you want, and the unwavering faith that you do get what you want, closing your mind against all that may tend to shake your purpose, dim your vision, or quench your faith.

That you may receive what you want when it comes, you must act NOW upon the people and things in your present environment.

Chapter 12
Efficient Action

YOU must use your thought as directed in previous chapters, and begin to do what you can do where you are, and you must do all that you can do where you are.

You can advance only be being larger than your present place; and no one is larger than his present place who leaves undone any of the work pertaining to that place.

The world is advanced only by those who more than fill their present places.

If no one quite filled his present place, you can see that there must be a going backward in everything. Those who do not quite fill their present places are dead weight upon society, government, commerce, and industry; they must be carried along by others at a great expense. The progress of the world is slowed only by those who do not fill the places they are holding. They belong to a former age and a lower stage or plane of life, and their tendency is toward degeneration. No society could advance if every man was smaller than his place; social evolution is guided by the law of physical and mental evolution. In the animal world, evolution is caused by excess of life.

When an organism has more life than can be expressed in the functions of its own plane, it develops the attributes of a higher plane, and evolution progresses upward to that higher place.

There never would have been new species had there not been organisms which more than filled their places. The law is exactly the same for you; your getting rich depends upon your applying this principle to your own affairs.

Every day is either a successful day or a day of failure, and it is the successful days which get you what you want. If every day is a failure, you can never get rich; if every day is a success, you cannot fail to get rich.

If there is something that may be done today, and you do not do it, you have failed insofar as that thing is concerned, and the consequences may be more disastrous than you imagine.

You cannot foresee the results of even the most trivial act; you do not know the workings of all the forces that have been set moving in your behalf. Much may be depending on your doing some simple act; it may be the very thing which is to open the door of opportunity to very great possibilities. You can never know all the combinations which Supreme Intelligence is making for you in the world of things and of human affairs. Your neglect or failure to do some small thing may cause a long delay in getting what you want.

Do, every day, ALL that can be done that day.

There is, however, a limitation or qualification of the above that you must take into account.

You are not to overwork, nor to rush blindly into your business in the effort to do the greatest possible number of things in the shortest possible time.

You are not to try to do tomorrow's work today, nor to do a week's work in a day.

It is really not the number of things you do, but the efficiency of each separate action that counts.

Every act is, in itself, either a success or a failure.

Every act is, in itself, either effective or inefficient.

Every inefficient act is a failure, and if you spend your life in doing inefficient acts, your whole life will be a failure.

The more things you do, the worse for you, if all your acts are inefficient ones.

On the other hand, every efficient act is a success in itself, and if every act of your life is an efficient one, your whole life must be a success.

The cause of failure is doing too many things in an inefficient manner, and not doing enough things in an efficient manner.

You will see that it is a self-evident proposition that if you do not do any inefficient acts, and if you do a sufficient number of efficient acts, you will become rich. If, now, it is possible for you to make each act an efficient one, you see again that the getting of riches is reduced to an exact science, like mathematics.

The matter turns, then, on whether you can make each separate act a success in itself. And this you can certainly do.

You can make each act a success, because all power is working with you; and all power cannot fail.

Power is at your service, and to make each act efficient you have only to put power into it.

Every action is either strong or weak, and when every one is strong, you are acting in the Certain Way which will make you rich.

Every act can be made strong and efficient by holding your vision while you are doing it, and putting the whole power of your faith and purpose into it.

It is at this point that the people who separate mental power from personal action fail. They use the power of mind in one place and at one time, and they act in another place and at another time. So their acts are not successful in themselves; too many of them are inefficient. But if all power goes into every act, no matter how commonplace, every act will be a success in itself. And as every success opens the way to other successes, your progress toward what you want, and the progress of what you want toward you, will come to you faster and faster.

Remember that successful action is cumulative in its results. Since the desire for more life is inherent in all things, when a person begins to move toward larger life more things attach themselves to her, and the influence of her desire is multiplied.

Do, every day, all that you can do that day, and do each act in an efficient manner.

In saying that, you must hold your vision while you are doing each act, however trivial or commonplace. I do not mean to say that it is necessary at all times to see the vision distinctly in its smallest details. It should be the work of your leisure hours to use your imagination on the details of your vision, and to contemplate them until they are firmly fixed upon memory. If you wish speedy results, spend practically all your spare time in this practice.

By continuous contemplation you will get the image of what you want, even to the smallest details, so firmly fixed upon your mind, and so completely transferred to the The Universal Mind, that in your working hours you need only to mentally refer to the picture to stimulate your faith and purpose, and cause your best effort to be put forth. Contemplate your image in your leisure hours until your consciousness is so full of it that you can grasp it instantly. You will become so enthused with its bright promises that the mere thought of it will call forth the strongest energies of your whole being.

Let us again repeat our main points, and by slightly changing the closing statements bring it to the point we have now reached.

There is a Universal Mind from which all things are made, and which, in its original state, permeates, penetrates, and fills the interspaces of the universe.

A thought produces the thing that is imaged by the thought.

Mankind can form things in its thought, and, by impressing its thought upon The Universal Mind, can cause the thing it thinks about to be created.

In order to do this, you must pass from the competitive to the creative mind; you must form a clear mental image of the things you want, and do, with faith and purpose, all that can be done each day, doing each separate thing in an efficient manner.

Chapter 13
Getting into the
Right Business

SUCCESS, in any particular business, depends upon your possessing in a well-developed state the skills and capabilities required in that business.

Without good musical capabilities no one can succeed as a teacher of music. Without well-developed mechanical capabilities no one can achieve great success in any of the mechanical trades. Without tact and good business capabilities no one can succeed in marketing pursuits. But to possess in a well-developed state the capabilities required in your particular vocation does not insure getting rich. There are musicians who have remarkable talent, and who yet remain poor; there are those who work in the trades who have excellent mechanical ability, but who do not get rich; and there are merchants with good skills for dealing with others who nevertheless fail.

The different skills are tools. It is essential to have good tools, but it is also essential that the tools should be used in the right way. One can take a sharp saw, a square, a good plane, and so on, and build a sturdy piece of furniture; another can take the same tools and set to work to duplicate the piece, but his project will be botched. It comes down to knowing how to use good tools in a successful way.

The various capabilities of your mind are the tools with which you must do the work which is to make you rich. It will be easier for you to succeed if you get into a business for which you are well equipped with mental tools.

Generally speaking, you will do best in that business which will use your strongest abilities, the ones for which you are naturally best fitted. But there are limitations to this idea. No one should regard his vocation as being irrevocably determined by the tendencies with which he was born.

You can get rich in any business, for if you do not have the right talents, you can develop those talents. It merely means that you will have to make your tools as you go along, instead of confining yourself to the use of those with which you were born. It will be easier for you to succeed in a vocation for which you already have the talents in a well-developed state, but you can succeed in any vocation, you can develop any rudimentary talent.

You will get rich most easily if you do that for which you are best fitted; but you will get rich most satisfactorily if you do that which you want to do.

Doing what you want to do is life, and there is no real satisfaction in living if we are compelled to be forever doing something which we do not like to do, and can never do what we want to do. And it is certain that you can do what you want to do; the desire to do it is proof that you have within you the power to do it.

Desire is a manifestation of power.

The desire to play music is the power which can play music seeking expression and development. The desire to invent mechanical devices is the mechanical talent seeking expression and development.

Where there is no power, either developed or undeveloped, to do a thing, there is never any desire to do that thing. And where there is strong desire to do a thing, it is certain proof that the power to do it is strong, and only requires to be developed and applied in the right way.

All things being equal, it is best to select the business for which you have the best developed talent. But if you have a strong desire to engage in any particular line of work, you should select that work as the ultimate end at which you aim.

You can do what you want to do, and it is your right and privilege to follow the business or vocation which will be the most pleasant and suited to you.

You are not obliged to do what you do not like to do, and you should not do it except as a means to bring you to the doing of the thing you want to do.

If there are past mistakes whose consequences have placed you in an undesirable business or environment, you may be obliged for some time to do what you do not like to do. But you can make the doing of it pleasant by knowing that it is making it possible for you to move toward what you want to do.

If you feel that you are not in the right vocation, do not act too hastily in trying to get into another one. The best way, generally, to change business or environment is by growth.

Do not be afraid to make a sudden and radical change if the opportunity is presented, and you feel after careful consideration that it is the right opportunity. But never take sudden or radical action when you are in doubt as to the wisdom of doing so.

There is never any hurry on the creative plane, and there is no lack of opportunity.

When you get out of the competitive mind you will understand that you never need to act hastily. No one else is going to beat you to the thing you want to do; there is enough for all. If one space is taken, another and a better one will be opened for you a little farther on; there is plenty of time. When you are in doubt, wait. Fall back on the contemplation of your vision, and increase your faith and purpose, and by all means, in times of doubt and indecision, cultivate gratitude.

A day or two spent in contemplating the vision of what you want, and in earnest thanksgiving that you are getting it, will bring your mind into such close relationship with The Universal Mind that you will make no mistake when you do act.

There is a mind which knows all there is to know, and you can come into close unity with this mind by faith and the determination to advance in life, if you have deep gratitude.

Mistakes come from acting hastily, or from acting in fear or doubt, or in forgetfulness of the right motive, which is more life to all, and less to none.

As you go on in the Certain Way, opportunities will come to you in increasing number; and you will need to be very steady in your faith and purpose, and to keep in close touch with The Universal Mind by reverent gratitude.

Do all that you can do in a perfect manner every day, but do it without haste, worry, or fear. Go as fast as you can, but never hurry.

Remember that in the moment you begin to hurry you cease to be a creator and become a competitor; you drop back upon the old plane again.

Whenever you find yourself hurrying, stop what you are doing. Fix your attention on the mental image of the thing you want, and begin to give thanks that you are getting it. The exercise of gratitude will never fail to strengthen your faith and renew your purpose.

Chapter 14
The Impression of Increase

WHETHER you change your vocation or not, your actions for the present must be those pertaining to the business in which you are now engaged.

You can get into the business you want by making constructive use of the business you are already established in, by doing your daily work in a Certain Way.

And insofar as your livelihood consists of dealing with other people in one way or another, the focus of all your efforts must be to convey to their minds the impression of increase.

Increase is what all men and all women are seeking; it is the urge of The Universal Mind within them, seeking fuller expression.

The desire for increase is inherent in all nature; it is the fundamental impulse of the universe. All human activities are based on the desire for increase; people are seeking more food, more clothes, better shelter, more luxury, more beauty, more knowledge, more pleasure, more life.

Every living thing needs continuous advancement; where increase of life ceases, dissolution and death set in at once.

People instinctively know this, and hence they are forever seeking more.

The normal desire for increased wealth is not an evil or a reprehensible thing. It is simply the desire for more abundant life. It is aspiration.

And because it is the deepest instinct of their natures, all men and women are attracted to those who can give them more of the means of life.

In following the Certain Way as described in the foregoing pages, you are getting continuous increase for yourself, and you are giving it to all with whom you deal.

You are a creative center, from which increase is distributed to all.

Be sure of this, and convey assurance of this fact to every man, woman, and child with whom you come in contact. No matter how small the transaction, even if it be only the selling of a stick of candy to a little child, put into it the thought of increase, and make sure that the customer is the recipient of the thought.

Convey the impression of advancement with everything you do, so that all people shall receive the impression that you are in a state of growth, and that you help all who deal with you to grow too. Even to the people you meet in a social way, without any thought of business, and to whom you do not try to sell anything, give the thought of increase.

You can convey this impression by holding the unshakable faith that you, yourself, are in a state of increase, and by letting this faith inspire, fill, and permeate every action.

Do everything that you do in the firm conviction that you are an advancing personality, and that you are giving advancement to everybody.

Feel that you are getting rich, and that in so doing you are making others rich, and conferring benefits on all.

Do not boast or brag of your success, or talk about it unnecessarily. True faith is never boastful.

Wherever you find a boastful person, you find one who is secretly doubtful and afraid. Simply feel the faith, and let it work out in every transaction. Let every act and tone and look express the quiet assurance that you are getting rich, and that you are already rich. Words will not be necessary to communicate this feeling to others; they will feel the sense of increase when in your presence, and will be attracted to you again.

You must so impress others that they will feel that by associating with you they will get increase for themselves. See that you give them a use value greater than the cash value you are taking from them.

Take an honest pride in doing this, and let everybody know it, and you will have no lack of customers. People will go where they are given increase, and The Universal Mind, which desires increase in all, and which knows all, will move toward you men and women who have never heard of you. Your business will increase rapidly, and you will be surprised at the unexpected benefits which will come to you. You will be able from day to day to build upon your successes, secure greater advantages, and to go on to a more congenial vocation if you desire to do so.

But doing all this, you must never lose sight of your vision of what you want, or your faith and purpose to get what you want.

Let me here give you another word of caution in regard to motives.

Beware of the insidious temptation to seek power over other people.

Nothing is so pleasant to the unformed or partially developed mind as the exercise of power or dominion over others. The desire to rule for selfish gratification has been the curse of the world all along. For countless ages kings and lords have drenched the earth with blood in their battles to extend their dominions, not to seek more life for all, but to get more power for themselves.

Today, the main motive in the business and industrial world is the same: men marshal their armies of dollars, and lay waste the lives and hearts of millions in the same mad scramble for power over others. Commercial kings, like political kings, are inspired by the lust for power.

Avoid for the temptation to seek authority, to become a master, to be considered as one who is above the common herd, to impress others by lavish display, and so on.

The mind that seeks mastery over others is the competitive mind; and the competitive mind is not the creative one. In order to master your environment and your destiny, it is not at all necessary that you should rule over your fellow men and indeed, when you fall into the world's struggle for the high places, you begin to be conquered by fate and environment, and your getting rich becomes a matter of chance and speculation.

Beware of the competitive mind!! No better statement of the principle of creative action can be made than this variation on the Golden Rule: "What I want for myself, I want for everybody."

Chapter 15
The Advancing Man

WHAT I have said in the last chapter applies as well to professionals and wage-earners as to businesspeople.

No matter whether you are a physician, a teacher, or clergy, if you can give increase of life to others and make them realize it, they will be attracted to you, and you will get rich. The physician who holds the vision of himself as a great and successful healer, and who works toward the complete realization of that vision with faith and purpose, will come into such close touch with The Universal Mind that he will be phenomenally successful, and patients will come to him in throngs.

No one has a greater opportunity to carry into effect the teaching of this book than the practitioner of medicine; it does not matter to which of the various specialties she may belong, for the principle of healing is common to all of them, and may be reached by all alike. Someone advancing in medicine, who holds to a clear mental image of herself as successful, and who obeys the laws of faith, purpose, and gratitude, will cure every curable case she undertakes, no matter what remedies she may use.

In the field of religion, the world cries out for clergy who can teach the true science of abundant life. Those who master the details of the science of getting rich, together with the sciences of being well, of being great, and of winning love, and who teaches these details from the pulpit, will never lack for a congregation. This is the gospel that the world needs; it will give increase of life, and people will hear it gladly, and will give wide support to the person who brings it to them.

What is now needed is a demonstration of the science of life from the pulpit. We want preachers who can not only tell us how, but who in their own persons will show us how. We need preachers who will be rich, healthy, great, and beloved, to teach us how to attain to these things. When they teach this, they will find a numerous and loyal following.

The same is true of the teacher who can inspire children with the faith and purpose of the advancing life. That teacher will never be out of a job. And any teacher who has this faith and purpose can give it to their pupils; they cannot help but give it to them if it is part of their own life and practice.

What is true of the teacher, preacher, and physician is true of the lawyer, dentist, real estate agent, insurance agent — of everybody.

The combined mental and personal action I have described is infallible; it cannot fail. Every man and woman who follows these instructions steadily, perseveringly, and to the letter, will get rich. The law of the Increase of Life is as mathematically certain in its operation as the law of gravity. Getting rich is an exact science.

The wage-earner will find this as true of his case as of any of the other professions mentioned. Do not feel that you have no chance to get rich because you are working where there is no visible opportunity for advancement, where wages are small and the cost of living high. Form your clear mental vision of what you want, and begin to act with faith and purpose.

Do all the work you can do, every day, and do each piece of work in a perfectly successful manner. Put the power of success, and the determination to get rich, into everything that you do.

But do not do this merely with the idea of currying favor with your employer, in the hope that he, or those above you, will see your good work and advance you. It is not likely that they will do so.

The person who is merely a good worker, filling their place to the very best of their ability, and satisfied with that, is valuable to their employer. But it is not in the employer's interest to promote that person; they are worth more where they are.

To secure advancement, something more than to be too large for your place is necessary.

The person who is certain to advance is the one who is too big for her place, and who has a clear concept of what she wants to be, who knows that she can become what she wants to be and who is determined to BE what she wants to be.

Do not try to more than fill your present place with a view to pleasing your employer; do it with the idea of advancing yourself. Hold the faith and purpose of increase during work hours, after work hours, and before work hours. Hold it in such a way that every person who comes in contact with you, whether a supervisor, a fellow worker, or a social acquaintance, will feel the power of purpose radiating from you and everyone will get the sense of advancement and increase from you. Others will be attracted to you, and if there is no possibility for advancement in your present job, you will very soon see an opportunity to take another job.

There is a power which never fails to present opportunity to the advancing person who is moving in obedience to law.

The Universal Mind cannot help but to assist you, if you act in a Certain Way; it must do so in order to help itself.

There is nothing in your circumstances or your situation that can keep you down. If you cannot get rich working in one business, you can get rich in another. And if you begin to move in the Certain Way, you will certainly escape from a dead-end path and get on to wherever else you wish to be.

If a few thousand employees would enter upon the Certain Way, any large corporation would soon be in a bad plight; it would have to give its workers more opportunity, or go out of business. Nobody has to work in a minimum-wage job that keeps people in so-called hopeless conditions only so long as there are people who are too ignorant to know of the science of getting rich, or too intellectually slothful to practice it.

Begin this way of thinking and acting, and your faith and purpose will make you quick to see any opportunity to better your condition.

Such opportunities will speedily come, for the Supreme, working in All, and working for you, will bring them before you.

Do not wait for an opportunity to be all that you want to be; when an opportunity to be more than you are now is presented and you feel impelled toward it, take it. It will be the first step, one of many, toward a greater opportunity.

There is no such thing possible in this universe as a lack of opportunities for you if you are living the advancing life.

It is inherent in the ways of the Universe that all things shall be for you and work together for your good; and you must certainly get rich if you act and think in the Certain Way. So let wage-earning men and women study this book with great care, and enter with confidence upon the course of action it prescribes. It will not fail.

Chapter 16
Some Cautions, and Concluding Observations

MANY people will scoff at the idea that there is an exact science of getting rich. Holding the impression that the supply of wealth is limited, they will insist that social and governmental institutions must be changed before even some people can become successful.

But this is not true.

It is true that existing governments keep the masses in poverty, but this is because the masses do not think and act in the Certain Way.

If the masses began to move forward as suggested in this book, neither governments nor economic systems can check them. All systems must change to accommodate the forward movement.

If people have the advancing mind, have faith that they can become rich, and move forward with the fixed purpose to become rich, nothing can possibly keep them in poverty.

Individuals may enter upon the Certain Way at any time, and under any type of government or economy, and make themselves rich. And when any considerable number of individuals do so under any government, they will cause the system to be so modified as to open the way for others.

The more men who get rich on the competitive plane, the worse for others; the more who get rich on the creative plane, the better for others.

The economic salvation of the masses can only be accomplished by getting a large number of people to practice the scientific method set down in this book, and become rich. These will show others the way, and inspire them with a desire for real life, with the faith that it can be attained, and with the purpose to attain it.

For the present, however, it is enough to know that neither the government under which you live nor the capitalistic or competitive system of commerce can keep you from getting rich. When you enter upon the creative plane of thought you will rise above all these things and become a citizen of a higher kingdom.

But remember that your thought must be held upon the creative plane; you are never for an instant to be betrayed into regarding the supply as limited, or into acting on the moral level of competition.

Whenever you do fall into old ways of thought, correct yourself instantly; for when you are in the competitive mind, you have lost the cooperation of the Mind of the Whole.

Do not spend any time in worrying about how you will meet possible emergencies in the future, except as the necessary policies may affect your actions today. You are concerned with doing today's work in a perfectly successful manner, and not with emergencies which may arise tomorrow. You can attend to them as they come.

Do not concern yourself with questions as to how you shall surmount obstacles which may loom upon your business horizon, unless you can see plainly that your course must be altered today in order to avoid them.

No matter how tremendous an obstruction may appear at a distance, you will find that if you go on in the Certain Way it will disappear as you approach it, or that a way over, through, or around it will appear.

No possible combination of circumstances can defeat a man or woman who is proceeding to get rich along strictly scientific lines. No man or woman who obeys the law can fail to get rich, any more than one can multiply two by two and fail to get four.

Give no anxious thought to possible disasters, obstacles, economic downturns, or unfavorable combinations of circumstances. There is time enough to meet such things when they present themselves before you in the immediate present, and you will find that every difficulty carries with it the wherewithal for its overcoming.

Guard your speech. Never speak of yourself, your affairs, or of anything else in a discouraging way.

Never admit the possibility of failure, or speak in a way that infers failure as a possibility.

Never speak of the times as being hard, or of business conditions as being doubtful. Times may be hard and business doubtful for those who are on the competitive plane, but they can never be so for you. You can create what you want, and you are above fear.

When others are having hard times and poor business, you will find your greatest opportunities.

Train yourself to think of and to look upon the world as a something which is becoming, which is growing, and to regard seeming evil as being only that which is undeveloped. Always speak in terms of advancement; to do otherwise is to deny your faith, and to deny your faith is to lose it.

Never allow yourself to feel disappointed. You may expect to have a certain thing at a certain time, and not get it at that time. This will appear to you like failure. But if you hold to your faith you will find that the failure is only apparent.

Go on in the Certain Way, and if you do not receive that thing, you will receive something so much better that you will see that the seeming failure was really a great success.

A student of this science had set his mind on making a certain business partnership which seemed to him at the time to be very desirable, and he worked for some weeks to bring it about. When the crucial time came, the arrangement failed in a perfectly inexplicable way. It was as if some unseen influence had been working secretly against him. He was not disappointed; on the contrary, he thanked God that his desire had been overruled, and went steadily on with a grateful mind. In a few weeks an opportunity so much better came his way, and he saw that The Universal Mind, which knew more than he knew, had prevented him from losing the greater good by entangling himself with the lesser.

That is the way every seeming failure will work out for you, if you keep your faith, hold to your purpose, have gratitude, and do, every day, all that can be done that day, doing each separate act in a successful manner.

When you fail, it is because you have not asked for enough; keep on, and a larger thing than you were seeking will certainly come to you. Remember this.

You will not fail because you lack the necessary talent to do what you wish to do. If you go on as I have directed, you will develop all the talent that is necessary to the doing of your work.

It is not within the scope of this book to deal with the science of cultivating talent; but it is as certain and simple as the process of getting rich.

However, do not hesitate or waver for fear that when you come to any certain place you will fail for lack of ability; keep right on, and when you come to that place, the ability will be provided to you. That same source of ability is open to you; you may draw upon all the mind there is for wisdom to use in meeting the responsibilities which are laid upon you. Go on in full faith.

Study this book. Read it over and over and over. Make it your constant companion until you have mastered all the ideas contained within. While you are getting firmly established in this faith, you will do well to give up your unproductive activities, and to stay away from places where ideas conflicting with these are promoted. Do not read pessimistic or conflicting literature, or get into arguments over the issue. Do very little reading outside of the writers mentioned in the Preface. Spend most of your leisure time in contemplating your vision, and in cultivating gratitude, and in reading this book. It contains all you need to know of the science of getting rich. You will find all the essentials summed up in the following chapter.

Chapter 17
Summary of
The Science of
Getting Rich

THERE is a Universal Mind from which all things are made, and which, in its original state, permeates, penetrates, and fills the interspaces of the universe.

A thought produces the thing that is imaged by the thought.

You can form things in your thought, and, by impressing your thought upon The Universal Mind, can cause the thing you think about to be created.

In order to do this, you must pass from the competitive to the creative mind; otherwise you cannot be in harmony with The Universal Mind, which is always creative and never competitive in spirit.

You may come into full harmony with The Universal Mind by entertaining a regular and sincere gratitude for the blessings it bestows upon you. Gratitude unifies our minds with the intelligence of The Universal Mind, so that our thoughts are received by The Universal Mind. You can remain in the creative plane only by uniting yourself with The Universal Mind through a deep and continuous feeling of gratitude.

You must form a clear and definite mental image of the things you wish to have, to do, or to become; and you must hold this mental image in your thoughts, while being deeply grateful to the Supreme that all your desires are granted to you. If you wish to get rich, you must spend your leisure hours contemplating this vision, and in earnest thanksgiving that this reality is being given to you. Too much stress cannot be laid on the importance of frequent contemplation of the mental image, coupled with unwavering faith and devout gratitude. This is the process by which the impression is given to The Universal Mind, and creative forces set in motion.

Creative energy works through the established channels of natural growth, and of the economic and social order. All that is included in your mental image will surely be brought to you if you follow the instructions given above, and if your faith does not waver. What you want will come to you through the ways of established trade and commerce.

In order to receive your own when it shall come to you, you must be active. This activity can only consist of more than filling your present place. You must keep in mind the determination to get rich through the realization of this mental image. And you must do, every day, all that can be done that day, taking care to do each act in a successful manner. You must give to every person a use value in excess of the cash value they receive, so that each transaction makes for more life. And you must so hold the advancing thought that the impression of increase will be communicated to all with whom you come in contact.

The men and women who practice the foregoing instructions will certainly get rich; and the riches they receive will be in exact proportion to the solidness of their vision, their determination, the steadiness of their faith, and the depth of their gratitude.

The End

Take Your Studies to a New Level

A startling statistic: 25% of American adults didn't read a single book last year! The astonishing thing about this is many of them brag about it! These are the people who are likely stuck in a place they don't want to be, making do with what they have, because they have neither the knowledge nor the will to advance their life.

There is only one way to gain a deeper understanding of yourself and how to advance your life — study! This is the only way to climb the ladder of success and move from one rung to the next.

Self-doubt, lack of confidence, and fear of what change will bring to your life come from your lack of knowledge on how to proceed with the changes you want to make, and a lack of understanding about how your mind works. When you attempt to make a change in your life, this lack of knowledge brings doubt and fear to your mind, which is then expressed by your body as anxiety. Your ability to think is the greatest gift you've ever received! What you want to do is study how your mind works, so you can use it to your advantage. Instead of doubt, fear, and anxiety, knowledge will bring you faith that you are able to accomplish your goals, even though at that point you may not see exactly how that will occur. But remember that what you need will be provided to you when you need it. This faith will be expressed as well-being, and you will feel at ease with your determination to make changes. This is the key to your ability to create.

By reading this book, you now have a basic understanding of how to start moving toward the life you want for yourself. Read and study this over and over until the ideas are second nature to you.

But there is more to be done on your journey. Hopefully this book has inspired you enough to take the next steps toward your goals.

You should make the next leap up the ladder of success by engaging with a coach or mentor to provide personal advice and guidance to make your dreams become reality. A coach helps keep you on track without falling by the wayside on the path to who you want to be. A good mentor facilitates the process and helps motivate you to get where you want to be as fast as possible. Links to a few suggested programs offered by the Proctor Gallagher Institute can be found at kingquantumthought.com. These excellent programs include:

THINKING INTO RESULTS FOR INDIVIDUALS

In-depth individual lessons focus intensively on a single essential element of the achievement process, with each lesson building upon the insights of the last.

Worksheets and activities challenge you to immediately apply what you learn, so you see and feel yourself changing, progressing, and moving closer to your goal in real time.

Dynamic videos viewed twice a day, morning and evening, motivate you and reinforce the lesson content at multiple levels of consciousness — a critical key to achieving change quickly and making it permanent.

60–90 minute live coaching/consulting sessions for each lesson give you the support, encouragement, answers, and expert guidance you need to keep moving forward on your journey to achievement.

Whether you know exactly what you want to achieve, or simply know that you want something more than what you currently have, *Thinking into Results* will open your mind to all you are capable of doing… then empower you to DO it.

THINKING INTO RESULTS FOR CORPORATIONS

The *Thinking Into Results* program includes:

Access to a highly-skilled and experienced Proctor Gallagher Institute Consultant, to guide and facilitate your team through the process.

A detailed and interactive curriculum that is proven to work for companies and teams of all sizes.

12 highly motivating lessons for leaders and their teams.

A detailed participant's guide with thought-provoking worksheets that drive results.

Overall Benefits: *Thinking Into Results* creates a culture that promotes employee growth in a positive environment where they feel supported and like they are a major contributor to the organization — no matter what position they hold. It allows your organization to create desired results without competing against others in your industry.

Six Minutes to Success

Dramatically increase your results in ALL areas of your life with the ease, convenience, and motivation of Six Minutes to Success. Get practical steps combined with the real inspiration you need to earn more money, create thriving relationships, start a wildly successful business, lose any amount of weight, and live a more productive, fulfilling life.

Magic in Your Mind

All The Success You've Ever Dreamed of … Magically Yours!

Now in a landmark coaching program, the Magic In Your Mind, Bob Proctor, Mary Morrissey, and Sandy Gallagher actually coach you on how to develop each of your six higher mental faculties — imagination, intuition, will, perception, memory, and reason.

The Proctor Gallagher Streaming Club

Mastermind and learn from the world's master thinkers and achievers each and every week!

We stream straight to you. The LIVE streaming sessions and recordings look great on all devices. So, whether you're on the go or in the comfort of your own home you can enjoy the Streaming Club stress free.

You may contact the author at:
jeffking.think@gmail.com

For *Thinking Into Results Consulting:*
didiking.think@gmail.com
www.kingquantumthought.com